TYING My SHOES

Stephen Redic

ISBN 979-8-88644-405-6 (Paperback)
ISBN 979-8-88644-406-3 (Digital)

Covenant Books
11661 Hwy 707
Murrells Inlet, SC 29576
www.covenantbooks.com

This book is dedicated in memory of my
brother, Al "Buddy" Robbins.

CONTENTS

GO AHEAD

Pick up your pen.
Feel that nervous energy start twitching
In your index finger, spreading to your thumb
Up your arm and into your mind—
Because that's where I am—your ideas—
And by the way, I'm in control.

Don't try to deny it, but if
You don't believe me, let me remind you
Of the facts.
How many times have you written
Something only to come back
A day later to total surprise
At the thoughts on the paper
With no clue as to how they got there,
Or how you got here?

Now, I will admit that you are a
Good editor, because I don't
Always worry about the details of a comma
Or the dilemma of a semi colon.
That spark of genius though,
That's me—not you.

You get all worried
About your inspiration drying up,
But it's just me taking a break.
While I'm recovering—you're

Out of luck, dumb, frontal lobotomy
Stupid, but then I wake up, and all of a sudden
You're a wonder. You're a writer.
You're a genius, a hero, a demon
A long squeeze of artificial lemon.
You are it.
Or is it me?
So go ahead.
Pick up your pen—I dare you.

TIME ON MY HANDS

When I was a child,
I had so much time on my hands,
I couldn't wash it all off.
The days were long,
And the nights were filled,
with dreams of tomorrow.

When I became a man,
The clock became my master,
The dollar my boss.
The days passed by in parade,
And the nights were short,
And void of dreams.

Now that I am ancient,
I count the minutes by seconds,
Give them names, a language of their own.
But all of our conversations are brief—
To the point.
The days are quickly night,
And the nights, the nights,
Are filled with dreams,
Of when I was young.

DOES YOGA MAKE YOU HUNGRY?

People in the park,
       Stretch their bodies—
Arms out—then above their heads—
Clearing negative energy,
       releasing positive chi.

Ripples of a nearby lake,
       Reflect
shafts of sunlight
Piercing
       clouds—
Each seeking
solace in another.

How happy are hands,
       that touch
one another
       above the head?
Or mother and child—
both grown older,
       learning to sit together
wrapped in silence?
Or runners who trade words for
       Footsteps
in the early morning forest air?
Do they eat their quiet

For breakfast or
        Save it for a later snack?

And if I write to you—
        because you are not here—
Are we as sailboats,
        floating at anchor,
Waiting for some captain
        to raise our sails?

SHARKS

I want to write a poem with a million words,
But that won't describe a single feeling.
I want to climb to the mountaintop,
But I'm afraid of heights.
I want to swim in the ocean,
But there are too many sharks, and I'm not hungry.
I want to fly to the sun and stars,
Instead, I'm a crash test dummy.
I want to paint a masterpiece,
But I'm color-blind and own a camera.

I want to be a knight in shining armor,
But I'm rusty and made of tin.
I want to find honesty,
But I only find fear.
I want to write a symphony,
That only dogs can hear.

I want Solitude to share her secrets,
But I don't know where she's hiding.
I want to know
Where we go
When we close our eyes,
But it's silent, dark, and deep.
I want to feel the dream inside of me,
While I pretend to sleep.

I want to hold your whispers,
Within my heart,
But I can only touch the echoes
Of your love.
I want to taste the sweet perfume,
Of our addiction,
But I can only breathe the heaven of your lips.
As the wind is howling,
Howling like a train whistle to a hobo's soul.
I want—but do not need.
I want.

ESCALATOR BOY

He wears a teal-colored
Angry Bird
Baseball cap
And a navy blue
"Boston Strong" hoodie
Over his Red Sox World Series T-shirt.

His perpetual smile
Is even larger
With his successful landing
At the top of the
Escalator—
Hands in the air
Fingertips
Outstretched
Reaching
For a gold medal
Only he can see.

After careful consideration
He approaches the
Down
     escalator like the
        edge
         of a cliff.

A quick snap of his head
And military
"About-face" turn
Reaffirms to the world
What he already knows—
He has made it to the top
And he isn't going down—just yet.

THE BALCONY

From the balcony window of the Hotel del Plaza,
You can look down at the market,
Where merchants in brightly colored stalls,
Sell to all for a price.
At the head of the street,
On the steps of the Mayor's Villa,
Two guitarists sit in the shade of lemon trees.

Dueling with fingers and strings,
They fight back and forth,
          Sliding
    From one fret to another,
Switching keys and changing leads,
Juggling themes and chords, like fire and chain saws.

In the finale, no one loses a finger,
As everyone applauds for payment,
And loose change makes,
That soft velvet tapping sound,
Searching for the bottom,
Of the empty guitar case.

ZOO

This is what it's like: people, people, people
Everywhere. They walk
And talk or scream and shout
Or laugh and cry.
At the mall, I watch them all
Listen to small snippets and bits of
Conversations lost in translations
With whispers and promises
That fade with the crowds as they walk away.
We feed on schedule
So we are present when they are here
But they just walk by
Without appreciating our hunger
Only making eye contact with the tile floor
Or the iPhone
That they hold like blind mice carrying a torch
To guide them to their friends
To the stores, to their cars
To their houses that await commands like:
Turn me on, make me bright, warm me up,
Lock my door, turn off my light.

This is what it must be like for
The animals in the zoo—
Waiting for everyone to stop
Pointing, to stop staring, to stop taking pictures.
Not the male silverback gorilla.
He climbs a tree

Turns his back to the crowd
And gives his best opinion
Of yesterday's meal.
A lady faints at the smell
While a small boy deposits
His lunch near the fountain.
Mr. Silverback throws his soiled leaves—
At the crowd—
Watches them scatter, hears them scream.
This is what it's like.
This is what it is.
Welcome to the zoo.

STREETLIGHT

It's not easy being a streetlight.
You don't get to pick your friends
Or the crowds you hang out with.
Did I mention I hate seagulls? And pigeons?
But from my vantage point, I get to see a lot.
I get to see Mr. Mercedes
Smoking a cigar, on his way to the golf
course and the nineteenth hole.
I get to see Mr. BMW, driving to meet Mrs. Mercedes
Perhaps they'll smoke later.
I get to see little Ms. white Toyota Camry meeting
Mr. Ford F-150 because
She likes his big, knobby tires and his four-wheel drive.
He likes the contour of her spoiler and her
High-beam headlights.
I even get to see Mrs. Blue Grand Caravan with
Her load of soccer going to the field.
Yeah, I can see there too.
It's where I first saw you.
Winking at me in the early dawn.
They said it wouldn't work—
After all, you're a private utility, and I'm
Public service, but sometimes things just happen.
I remember the last time I saw you,
You were coughing up sparks
Like the Universe
Giving birth to the stars, then you went dark.
I don't look in that direction much anymore.

I mostly look down.
There, I see the glassy eyes of the homeless
Staring up at me
From the shelter of a cardboard box—
Like I was some kind of salvation.
Together we drink the early morning colors
like sweet communion wine
And we drink, and we drink, and we drink—until I am drunk
In black-and-white—and I still can't forget you.
Now, my only friends are the moths.
They think I'm brilliant.

WALKING IN PAIRS

Some walk in pairs—
Holding each other up,
Remembering,
"Where are we going?"
Caring as long as possible.

Some sit by windows,
Staring at the nothing,
Trying to remember,
What it was like to walk,
To talk,
To be free.

Some walk alone,
With two,
Almost good legs,
On missions for a spouse,
That passed a year ago.
Sleep won't come
Into an
Empty space,
And the sound
Of one heartbeat
Is loudest in the
Silence of the night.

That's when I think of you,
And how we walked together,
Like nothing mattered—or ever would.

When you asked for my help,
I couldn't say no.
I put the medication close to you
And left the room.
How was I to know you wouldn't save
Any for me?

DAYS

For days I walk alone,
On these desert roads of dirt and stone.
I become dry, brittle, and
When the wind blows,
    I shatter, crumbling
to pieces,
like leaves,
deserting trees
after the first frosty kiss of fall.
The wind carries me,
Tumbling, twisting, turning—
Depositing some of me
        against this
rock: Or that bush,
until I become a single speck of dust—
rising to the sky, swirling in a vortex.
When the wind becomes bored with me,
    I am released.
Landing near nowhere,
I stand in the shade of Saguaro cacti,
watching the day running away from the sky.
Crows land beside me.
They become old women, dressed in black satin
with fine Spanish lace.
They smile,
    offer me their charms,
    suggestions, directions.

The comfort
        of their outstretched arms.
Shaking my head, I refuse, because
I've already been—
Everywhere, they want me to go.
Everything, they want me to be.

TYING MY SHOES

Take two ends, cross, pull tight,
Bunny loop, bunny loop,
Pull tight and even,
Now take a walk.
It's easy, you never forget.

I wake, take two ends,
Pull tight, bunny loop, bunny loop,
Pull tight, one loop slips,
Now it's a knot, so I take a walk.
It's easy, you never forget.

Now where am I?
I came in here for something?
You never forget.
Take one end, bunny loop,
Take another end, pull tight,
It's okay, I made a knot, now another
Because the ends are too long.
Knot, not too short, take a walk.
Take two ends, pull tight.
Now what, which end,
Goes where,
        I take a walk.
    Laces loose,
I talk to them, so we are friends,
And I don't fall.

Take two ends,
Like time starting and stopping in my hands,
Pull tight,
Bunny what?
Cross them over, cross them over,
Knot, knot, cross them
No wait, take a walk.
I don't care.
Where am I now? Who are you?

ISABELLA—AN AFTERNOON AT THE MUSEUM

Required: walking, waiting, watching, as
The cascade of time falls away
    Like the gentle folds of the tapestries
    Hanging on the wall.
If you're listening:
    You can hear dogs bark
    In faded marketplace scenes—
    Stitched three hundred years ago.
You can imagine the rising hum of conversation
    Sprinkled with high pitched giggles
    Between the *Ooh*s and *Aah*s
    Of children playing.
Like water bubbling up in the circular fountain.
There are letters left from the dead,
in flourishes of quill pen enthusiasm,
locked in the throes of embellishment.
Calligraphy wrestles
grammar, connotation, and punctuation,
    in a fight to the finish.

There are signatures of the famous.
Photographs of people starting to fade.
Etchings, sketches, and paintings
by the masters or their students.
All begging to be part of the present, the future,
the maybe of the unknown past.

Then, there is the smell.
That locked away in a trunk, shipped across the ocean,
    stored out of sight for years—smell.
Curiosity, old houses, and museums
    all smell the same.
Like time, water, and old wood.

GREAT

I have seen:
The "greatest," The "goat,"
The "undefeated,"
The first perfect ten,
A World Series overcome,
By an earthquake and,
Football played in fog.

I have seen records for home runs, hits, and RBIs,
Pitching dominance measured in mph and the letter *K*,
I have seen Super Bowls—all of them.
I have seen Larry Legend, Bill Russell,
Orr and Esposito,
Yaz, Clemens, and Pedro,
And yes, Brady and Belichick:
I am from New England.

I can't feel anything but humble and lucky,
Because when I say, "I had a dream,"
It was real.
All these heroes took me to a mountaintop,
Where, for just a moment,
I could see something—
Something better—
Like you deserved your next breath,
Earned your victory by hard work, sweat, and determination,
Accomplished a dream, saved the world,
Became a champion.

All accomplished with the same simple joy,
Of a small child freeing dandelion's snow-colored seeds,
Like small helicopters,
Into the wind, into the future.

IN THE SILENCE

In the silence,
	Whispers of God
Echo in all things.
	In the silence,
A common spark
Makes us human beings.

In the silence,
You can feel the tide
Surging across
Barren beaches of soul.
In the silence,
You can breathe in the stars
	Of a million Milky Ways,
While feeling sorry for the loneliness
	Of black holes.

In the silence,
	You can hear heartbeats
Carried by cool night air.
Carried into dreams—suspending time
	While reality demands its share.

In the silence,
You can tell the truth
And never speak.
In the silence,
You can listen with your heart

Laugh with your eyes,
And dance in your sleep.

In the silence,
You can have all the quiet
You can keep.

THE DOOR

Opens
   A crack.
Small sliver of outside framed in
Shadowbox perfection.
Against inside darkness
It fights for space.

My attention
Is on
The smoky gray cat,
Long tail.
        Curling
      Around
   The edge
Of the door.

She glides in—
All green-eyed curiosity—
Humpurring her satisfaction,
At having made a grand
Entrance.
She sits like a statue,
      With only
The tremor
      Of a tail
To betray
      Her impatient beast.

TALKING TO CARS

Hey! Watch out—damn Masshole!
In a hurry—go find me a cop.
Tailgating like drafting at NASCAR—
Cutting off the car in front,
Foot to the floor, full throttle, pedal in the down position.

But have you done the math?
Going seventy-five instead of sixty-five
Will only get you there ten seconds
Before never.
Eighty-five is faster but
Won't outrun the
Radar.
Ninety-five is flying
Until someone going sixty-five pulls in front
Of you and the
Application of brakes isn't
In your vocabulary or rearview mirror.
Because at 139 feet per second, stuff happens—
Stuff people don't anticipate—cause and effect—
One foot in front of the other.

Because, sometimes you just don't know.
You just don't know.
How an argument can be the last words shared.
How those words can cause the muscles in your right foot,
To cramp and push the accelerator to the floor,
As the ringing in your ears is an echo of the tightness in your chest,

The shortness of your breath.
The redness in your face is a reflection of
the tail lights in front of you.
Switching lanes between determination and
destiny, you race down a road
To nowhere,
Running from the truth that's driving by, lights
flashing, siren singing your song.
You can't drive like this for long
Without reaching a destination,
You never knew you were going to.

Hey! Was that car invented before signals?
Or would that just be a sign of weakness?

HOW TO PRESENT

Carefully select each word.
Apply bubble wrap.
Words are delicate,
Like blown glass hummingbirds,
Hovering over crystal petals.

Box carefully with connotations,
Vocal intonations, and implications,
Intact, inexact, victims of interpreted fact.

Drape on paper,
Precisely cut, perfectly folded,
Invisibly sealed,
          Edges,
Forming angles,
      And associations,
        With infinite planes,
          Like bridges over water.
Connecting two islands of thought:
Yours and mine:
Igniting volcanoes of curiosity,
Releasing imagination's velocity,
          Leaping from one word to the next.
Playing games with surprise,
Solving mysteries with our eyes.

We hold them close, those words—
Like soft velvet robes,
Snuggle in their scent, feel their comfort,
Attach them to our dreams—
Like diamonds around the moon's neck—
            Signs in a midnight sky.

ESCALATOR PEOPLE

Riding the
    Up/down stairs
        They text the ones
            Next to them or across
                The mall or at home
                    Or while driving—
                        Though they have
                        Been warned
                            By beeping horn and
                              Flashing lights, saying,
                                "Drive to survive"
                          But all that changes nothing
                    Because staying connected to the herd
              Offers the greatest chance to LOL or LMAO
          Or LOLA by the kinks
        As the gods of Google play trivial pursuit
        With fastest thumbs
       Banging their way through universes
    They know nothing about—except with that new app
The one that only works on the down escalator
              And will automatically like us on Facebook.
          Watch your step!

MIND OVER MATTERS

They say I've lost my mind
But that implies an ownership
I've never had or wanted.
As for "crazy," I'm confused—
My ADD diagnosis assigns a deficit
To my attention: when the truth is closer
To having an overabundance of attention.
Everything is interesting all at once!

I get lost in thought
On my way to a perceived reality
Like as if the squirrel can hear me muttering
"Don't you dare!"
As he decides if suicide
Is worth crossing the road for.
The chickens know the answer, but
They're too busy with
The falling sky to explain why.

I stand on the edge of a giant circle,
Stunned by perception,
Swallowed by perfection,
A tangent to every point, every direction.

Without cognition,
Falling trees would have no voice,
The sky would have no color,
The moon would know no love,

And I would still be lost—
Thinking of you, thinking of you,
Thinking of you and me.

MOONLIGHT

When moonlight is:
All you drive by is:
Obscured by clouds is:
A sign that signs are coming and it is:
Like a thousand hurricanes ripping
Mountains
From my heart—like landslides that crumble
Down to the sea—touching the shores of your soul.
You retreat before the tide,
Only feeling a few drops of spray shared with salt,
And rocks that peek at horizons.
Horizons where the moon sits after a long night's work—
Sweeping skies of unseen stars,
Stars that are like memories.
Like my heart remembers you,
Each star—
With its own set of twinkles,
Its own set of wishes.

WHEN TO LOVE

I might love,
When the first flicker of dawn fades
To the last low whispers of dusk as
She kisses the day "good night," sleep well.
I might love you then.

I could love,
When the moon rises, folds the night aside
Like the deep velvet curtains of an old vaudeville stage—
Stars burning in the footlights like candles at the altar.
I could love you then.

I should love,
When our laughter
Echoes over the lake
Sunshine reflecting our embrace
In ripples, whitecaps, and waves.
I should love you then.

I shall love,
Even in the quiet times—
When we sit and forget together
When your smile is the only name I can remember
When your heartbeat is all I feel
Then, then I will love—
Then, I will love you.

FIRST TIME

When first we love,
The night will be clear
So the stars may watch,
And the moon may envy our warmth,
Jealous of the Sun.

When first we love,
We shall be as the ocean
Moaning over the sand,
Littered with footprints.
Surging back and forth
Sharing motion with emotion,
We sway back and forth like the tide.

When first we love, we shall be as fire.
Our imaginations will dance together,
Soaring like sparks, like gypsies in the dark,
Our freedoms unfettered.

When first we love, we will be music,
Sharing the blues beat with the pulse
In the palms of our hands—so eager the touch.
There shall be laughter,
And the sky will answer in chorus.
We will open ourselves as books,
Savoring the fragrance of every page
We turn by a tattered edge.

When last we love, I shall arrive late,
Rumbling like a freight train dressed in black.
You will know me by my kiss.
In the silence of our secret garden,
In the quiet of our dreams,
We will breathe. We will love.

WHAT I WANTED TO
WRITE ABOUT

I wanted to write something
That you would remember
So completely
That you could repeat
The words—
Slipping them into
Conversations
Unnoticed—
Like a mickey in a sailor's drink
Leaving listeners in wonder
Always wanting more.

I wanted to write about the weather.
How, because of its constant change
That we admired it
Or cursed it
Or sat in speechless wonder.
Staring at the tides of clouds
Washing over a shore we cannot reach.
I wanted to write about change but
My words are obsolete
Before my pen
Touches paper.
I wanted money for my ideas—
Only to find I couldn't give them away.
So I wanted to write them down

For when parts of me aren't working
And I will want to, need to,
Remember.

I wanted to write something for you
Something that would make you smile.
I really just wanted to say, "I love you"
So
I just wanted
To write
Before I forget.
I just wanted to write.

AGENTS OF DESIRE

We sit on park benches,
Facing opposite ways.
We never look at each other,
Even as we exchange
Instructions or a package.

We whisper, only loud enough,
For the squirrels to hear.
Listen and repeat:
No paper trails to betray.

Sometimes, on a train,
I stand and sway
Back and forth.
You always approach from behind.
Slowly slipping
Your hand into my pocket—
Teasing me
Before I turn—and you are gone.
I close my eyes remembering,
The lingering touch of your perfume.

At the hotel bar
My favorite cocktail waits
Guarding a napkin
Full of names, dates,
And coordinates
To nowhere, for no one.

The tab is paid for by a
Blonde/redhead/brunette—
Who just left.

The messages we carry—-we never read.
They say nothing that matters to us.
Nothing that poets will write about.
Nothing the shadows will repeat.
Nothing.

I WILL NOT SAY

I will not say, "I'm sorry,"
If I tell you
That you're beautiful.
Nor will I be to blame,
When in the silence,
I repeat your name.

I will not care
What music plays,
Nor blame bad luck and chance,
As long as you are in my arms,
For the final dance.

I will not wish
For more than this:
A precious moment's gift,
A smile upon your face,
Laughter on your lips,
And a simply sinful kiss.

I will not say, "I'm sorry,"
If I steal
Your last goodbye.
I will not say I failed,
If I didn't try.
I will not turn away,

When in your eyes I stare.
I will just say,
"I love you,"
Just because I dare.

DRACULA'S FIRST LOVE

She arrives:
Carried by strong hands,
    weak minds,
and fears of dark desire.
They recite pledges to the unseen,
    Cross their hearts,
    hurrying,
between
    falling
        raindrops,
Returning:
        like sparks to the safety of fire.

        I feel no such urgency,
for she shall wait,
            as my crowbar key
            unlocks all eternity.
When they find the
    vacant
        mahogany,
their fear
        will feed the worms,
become the conversations of crows.

        Our first embrace
is filled
        with empty.

Our first kiss
          is a feast of forever.
We do not know
          the difference
between our hunger and our thirst.
Only the musky scent of love,
our fear of fire,
          and the horror
          of a sunrise we can never see.

VENICE

The breakwaters of the old lagoon
Are lined with the gondolas
Used for the tourists.
The square clock tower and the Doge's palace
Are in the background near the
Piazza del San Marco, where
All who visit Venice must pass through.
The Golden Dome of Saint Mark's
Is a symbol of the wealth that built the city.

The gondolas rock back and forth
In a swaying rhythm
Learned from lovers
Floating through canals
Sighing under bridges.
The plush red crushed/velvet seats
Are deliberately intimate
Ideal for conversations
Secrets of inspiration
Whispers of dedication.

The gondolier
Sings in a language
The lovers do not understand.
Takes his time
Paddles slowly
Because he knows
The tip will be better.

WAKE UP

Moist lips
in full
anticipation of a kiss,
barely brushing
against
your neck,
swept under your skin
with whisper's broom,
a lover's exhale
of excitement.

Completely cocooned,
You become
    the rhythm.
    exhaling
until there's nothing left.
Now inhale
all that is around you:
The smell of coffee
means morning,
like the sizzle of bacon.
Next
to the scrambling eggs,
accompanies the popping sound
      of toaster.
      It raises your head out of pillow,
for just a second until
you surrender to what matters.

Lay back down into
fluffy morning moments.
Close your eyes. Exhale.

RED LIGHT

Our eyes meet,
Say, "Hello,"
Have drinks,
Get drunk,
Make love,
Say goodbye.
All
In
Rearview
Mirrored glances.

Green light!
She is right
And I,
Am left.

ALMOST SIX

I'm almost six,
Anxious to be seven.
What I don't know isn't
As important as what I do.
I know I can be anything:
Even a pro baseball player,
Or a millionaire with a mansion,
Or a magician with a rabbit,
Or a superhero dragon slayer,
With my own comic book and a cool costume.

I can kiss a girl—just not right now,
Or run real fast and win a gold medal.
Feel the wind in my face,
Fly a kite,
Eat anything—not green,
Paint with my fingers,
Color outside the lines.

Slide on the grass,
Ride my bike anywhere—except in the street,
Play with my friends or my dog,
Watch cartoons and laugh until my stomach hurts,
Swim until I can only float,
Eat more hotdogs than my sister,
Make her scream with my frog!

I'm almost six—
And it's the best!

BASEBALL

This is my affection, my affliction,
My connection to direction.
It's 132 beats per second,
Of my heart's anticipation
Of wild syncopation like
Beethoven's question
In silent persuasion.

That single moment,
Suspended in the hiss,
Transformed by the magic of the announcer's kiss.
Something like this:
The count is three and two, tie score,
Bottom of the ninth.
Bases loaded with two out.
The pitcher looks in and gets the sign,
He sets.
Here's the windup, the pitch…
And all you're thinking is,
"Don't strike out."
But everyone strikes out,
Even the "Babe" or Ted or Hank,
Because baseball is about dealing with failure.
So what are you going to do?

Whine at a called strike three
On the outside corner at the knees,
Or swing at a ball in the dirt with

First base practically free.
Or will you swing for the fence,
Where seams and dreams
Become one
With the "sweet"
Spot
Of your bat.
It's a line drive, a deep fly ball,
A real blast if it stays fair…
Way back, back, back…
And for an instant,
Everyone is quiet.

AT THE EDGE OF THE EVENT HORIZON:

Is a feeling like musical notes following each other—
not to the end of a song, only to the next note,
the same song that Moses hears,
gazing at the promised land,
or Joan of Arc as she stares at the sky,
at God, above the flames at her feet,
or Amelia as she kisses the ocean goodbye.
Her eyes open to the distant horizon,
or Jackie as she holds John's hand and smiles,
one last time in Dallas,
or Dr. King as he wakes from a dream,
and walks to the hotel balcony,
for a breath of fresh air,
or Christie as she feels the surge of boosters,
and the gentle roll of the challenger.

In my dream,
we are voices just
barely forming breezes
making treetops sway.
I smell a morning, I cannot see.
Sing to clouds I cannot touch.
Feel a bass line in a
Mississippi blues riff
that makes me listen
makes me tap—my—toe

lets me taste
the melt
of
ice cream
on a hot August day.

LAKESIDE

Yesterday,
You were all whitecap angry,
Swearing in lightning,
Pounding fists of hail,
Crying in the cold rain.

Today,
You are a mirror of antique glass,
A reservoir of calm,
A lover's face,
Reflecting radiant lines of supplication,
Reaching for random thoughts,
Gliding like boats,
Across the surface of imagination.

Tomorrow,
You will shine like a million suns.
I will gather you up like diamonds,
As my heart elopes,
To your opposite shore.

Together,
We will stare at the sky,
Color with our imaginations,
Become silver dreams:
Waiting for the moon,
To gather us up,
Take us home.

IN THE QUIET

I listen to heartbeats/
    Not my own.
They insert themselves/
    Between
whispers of wind—
Change direction/
    under silent wings.

My night hunter eyes,
    too large
    For daytime glare,
At twilight's touch—
    They sit and stare.

    Focus on distant/
    commotion
caused by motion/
    Fleeing time/
fleeting notion.

My eyes decide
    If "when" tastes better
Than "never,"
    Or if the "present"
Needs spice—
    to make it worth the ride.

When my hunger takes flight,
It trades altitude for speed,
Silence for shadows,
Talons for mercy,
Quiet for the night.

MARLBORO MAN

Death is like the Marlboro Man.
Riding into town on a pair of Colt 45s
His spurs dance with the dust as he strides into
The center of the street.
From a distance, he's just a vague shadow on the horizon
But at ten paces, he's a giant!
With eyes like mirrors that never blink, and we—
We're just reflections of what he thinks.
The ticktock of the tower clock
Punctuates a sentence you're already serving,
As the high noon sweat
Soaks your shirt into the shape of a cross.
Your hands are shaking, and your breath is shallow
And your heart, your heart, you never heard it beat so loud.
But Death's hand is steady,
Having been here before—again and again.
And in the end, Death cheats.
Because you see, Death is a golden butterfly,
Floating in a deep blue sky, on an invisible wind.
Her kiss is so gentle
You'll barely even notice.

MAVERICK

Meteor rides,
gravity's horse,
Bronco—hand—in air,
tossed before the final
bell,
exploding across
midnight sky,
A requiem for
dinosaurs.

We are almost
at the edge
        before the fall,
almost at the silence
        before the final note,
Almost at the remembering
of what it was like
before.

This moment—is nothing without you.
This next instance—I cannot bear.
Beyond this—is the edge of a universe
I cannot imagine.

How do stars fill my vision
When the galaxy is so empty?
    How is love
suppose to fill

the spaces
between
all the broken pieces?
And if it does,
is it a supernova,
or just the other side
of darkness?

THE DEVIL AND FIRE

When he sees her
She takes his breath away
Like a ticket for a carnival ride.
She calls herself innocent—
Living on moonlight and
The folly of forever.
She dances like a shadow in the dark.

When she sees him
His smile is an invitation.
His laughter is like music.
He calls himself promise—
But never keeps his word.
He shares secrets with
Cheap wine and wafers
Confessions with orphans.

When they whisper to each other
She calls him Prometheus—
He calls her Eve.
She sets him free—
He crumbles and turns to ash.

He learns from his scars
That he cannot hold her.
She is the sky he can see—but never touch.
She learns to listen with her heart.
When he is near—
It sounds like the rain
On a tin roof.

AT THE BOTTOM
OF THE ALTAR

The sun is swallowed by
A greedy moon,
Until full with night's darkness,
    Overflowing
    with
Pregnant pause,
      she smiles at her
Accomplishments.
      Ah-Cun-Can, you
      charmer of serpents.

Her reflected radiance
    Shares the blindness of night
With dawn's starving stars,
    Scattered through heaven
Like breadcrumbs for birds.
They flicker, becoming pale
      and full of envy.
      The sun gods—
Apollo, Helios, Sunna, Surya, Kinich Ahau—
Together, they
      slip slumber's grip,
Shake the sleep off the earth
    through cascades of color.
Smile at us—radiance pure,
Until we remember not to stare.

At the bottom of the altar,
        Dancing like whitecaps on water—
            Dazzling in our worship,
                Of the sun's returns—
                    We sing,
                        We rejoice,
                            We live.

RED

Hi, there, I'm the apple.
I see you,
Staring at me like that.
Is my fruit hanging low,
Or do you just think I'm easy?
Don't say anything, I might blush.
Not that you'd notice—
Red is my natural color.

Then, there's the way
You run your fingers
Over my firm, shiny, skin.
Tugging, twisting, turning,
Until I surrender my grip on this tree of knowledge
And come into your eager hand.

Snake warned me about this
But I'm not corn, I don't have ears.
I didn't listen.
He told me you would betray us—
Sharing me with "him!"
How could you?
He thinks he's so smart:
Naming animals, giving orders,
Making sacrifices.

Wait until he gets a taste of me:
I'll enlighten him.

He'll finally see
How beautiful you really are.
Then, we'll see who hides
Behind the fig leaves.
I can't wait for lunch.

OPEN LETTER TO EVE

My dearest one and only,
I remember the first time we met.
I woke up sore, like I had broken a rib.
(Maybe I fell out of a tree while I was sleeping)
But there you were—perfect in so many ways.
You laughed at my stories and followed me everywhere.
We used to play the "name the new animal" game even
Though you were better at it than me.
(How did you ever come up with platypus anyway?)
That's why when you offered me a new fruit
(you called it an apple?—cute)
I didn't think twice—just took a bite.
Now everything has changed.
We're getting evicted, and I have to get a new job.
(I can be a gardener anywhere) but you—
You've put on weight lately and gotten awfully cranky,
Not to mention those cravings.
(I can't get you ice cream when I don't
know what it is.) Then—boom!
It happens—those things you call tears. Now, I'm
looking for an all-night convenience store.
Oh well, I just wish that things could be the way they used to be,
When I would hold your hand at night,
and everything would be quiet.
When it was just you, me, and the snake—alone in the garden—
Watching angels fall like stars.

KATANA

Battered by hammer,
Tempered by the forge,
Folded inward and over,
One thousand times.

Sharpened edge,
Like a polished tongue,
Cuts deeply,
Into the drumming/heartbeats.

Bands pass by
Leaving empty
Barricades.
Pale-skinned
Mannequins
Wave goodbye/hello
To pigeons scattering
The daily news.

Coffee cups race
Past
The gang of squirrels.
They own the park
By chattering,
"My territory!"
To anyone listening.

Darkness
Tells the poet,
"It's almost tomorrow.
Look at the sky!
Be quiet now."

MY PEN SERVES PAPERS

My pen has served papers on me—
Orders restraining me from writing—
Especially with other pens—until such time
As deemed appropriate by the court.

Granted, I've been in a dry spell recently,
But that's no reason to start with the incriminations.
The charges are numerous such as
Too much pressure—I thought the pen meant
I was pushing down on the paper too hard—
She's very protective of paper—
Instead, she says I'm just too intense—
Writing in the present,
Using descriptive adjectives and adverbs,
And such a loose cannon with my punctuation.
Then there's the matter of my handwriting—
Everything I used to write in a beautiful cursive,
Now, I print.
Worse—I allegedly use a computer.
My pen feels this is a blatant example of infidelity—
Not to mention those hot steamy passages
Written with what seems like my left hand,
Almost illegible—What was I thinking?

Then, there's all the downtime.
I try to explain that
After our last writing session—
I thought she was out of ink.

I am promptly informed that just because I'm done with a pen and
I see a little ink blot doesn't mean that my pen is done.
That, combined with being left alone out in the car,
In the cold, cold night,
And well—
Things don't look so good for me when it comes to my defense.
So for now, my pen is refusing to write and
I am left all, backed up with ideas.
Does anyone have a pencil I could borrow?

TO MY FATHERS

I want to write a poem that tells,
About the hero in my dad,
And how he got old and tired,
And lay down on the living room floor,
Because of the pain in his back.
That was his heart exploding.
Arriving at the hospital,
I remember the fear in my mother's voice as we were ushered into a
side room.
I insisted on seeing the body like I could raise the dead,
Change the truth.

Almost twenty years later,
I met my biological father.
Bought him a drink, made him laugh,
At a bad joke.
I wanted to write about how we became friends,
But that wasn't the way it went.
I remember my brother,
Doing his duty, holding him down,
So he couldn't pull the IV out,
As doctors sedated those last hours,
To keep him "calm."

With both of them, though, what
I remember most is the sound of the
Bugle playing taps.
That melody still plays

In my head;
And even though I know the ending,
I listen. Listen
all the way to the last note.
Listen for the echo.
Close my eyes,
Catch my unnoticed tears,
Listen to the silence: the silence
Between heartbeats: the silence
Between father, between son, the silence.
Listen. Just listen.

4 PARROTS

When you look at me,
Do you only see my bright colors,
Or hear my call echo through the jungle?
I am a sum of generations.

My great grandfather sits over/above my shoulder,
The same way he sat on his master's shoulder—
A pirate sailing among the leeward islands.
He flew high and proud—never once repeating the directions,
To a treasure only men would seek.
As the captain danced his final jig on yardarms gallows.

My grandfather was a free bird—
Feeding himself fat on nuts and grubs.
He never heard the dart that stopped his heart,
Becoming an adornment for a warrior's shield,
A warrior's pride.

My father was captured while I was still in nest,
He went to sea though he could not swim.
He paced back and forth upon his perch
Aboard ship called the "Arizona."
When the bombs began to fall,
He died screaming, "Who's on first! What's on second!"
Because the sailors liked that and always laughed.

I will never learn to speak, nor sit on a man's shoulder.
When I fly, I will fill in the sky.

With the colors of my ancestors—
Their hopes in my songs, their dreams in my eyes.
Their freedom in my flight, on my wings.
I will never learn to speak.
Never.

SILVERSMITH

When the strangers come,
They smile and share stories
Of places they have seen.
It is always the same way
Because they are filled with want
And will not leave me
until they empty themselves—
replacing desire with silver.

I replace sleep with the
Empty
They leave behind.
Fashion dreams for them to wear,
Make my hands busy with details
too small to be important.
I shape, fold,
And fasten their attention
On a world they do not notice.

When I finish,
They only see
Beauty—
They cannot imagine.
Shapes,
They cannot form.
Thoughts,
They cannot own.

When I dream,
I fly to the in-between.
I walk outside myself.
I swim inside volcanoes.
I cover myself in silver.
I reflect on the world.

SEBASTIAN

Sebastian's my name,
Sweet like sugar cane.
My sunburned back bends to worship
The dollar I lack.
I laugh all day to make the pain go away.
I cry at night, when
No one can see.

Sebastian likes the girls.
They like him back.
Like to dance and drink, tell the joke.
Like to drink and sing and have a smoke.
Sebastian's my name,
Sweet like sugarcane.

When I was sixteen,
I believed my ancestors ruled Atlantis
And I was a prince.
When I turned seventeen,
I met Marie.
She showed me her voodoo.
I become her walking dead.
When I turn twenty-one,
I escape and run—
A stowaway with offset hat
And a white T-shirt
I never own before.

In America, I look
Like all the others.
Lose my way, travel north,
Follow crops or weather.
Around my neck,
I carry her photo
Framed inside a silver heart.
I never open it
And never will.
Sebastian's my name,
Sweet like sugarcane.

EL TORO

He is my little bull, "El Toro,"
And one day, he will be a man.
He will grow up strong and
One day, he will be a matador.
With final thrust.
He will kill the bull—
He will be a man.

In my arms,
He sleeps
In sunshine slumber—
Because he is weak from hunger:
Because we have no money:
Because we have no food.

One day,
He will be strong.
He will be a man.
He will be a matador.
He will kill the bull
And maybe the Fascists
Who give us guns,
Or the socialists who wish to share,
Or the communists, or the democrats.
He will kill them all.
Kill them all for me.

He will be a man.
He will be a matador.
He will kill the bull.

THE DANCE

All day, all night,
She kneels.
White tile, black tile,
She scrubs.

Gray water—
Blood of Christ.
Tattered rag,
Body of Christ.
White tile, black tile,
Holy Spirit.

She washes away,
Footsteps to the altar,
Sacraments reborn.
She washes away,
Footsteps to confessional,
Forgiveness renewed.
She washes away,
Footsteps to the last pew,
Never too late.

She washes away,
Footsteps of friends,
Denial of sanctuary.
She washes away the,
Footsteps of Fascists,
Judas's betrayal.

She washes away everything,
But the footsteps of the children.
Their tears remaining, staining, blaming.

She washes away her sins,
In footsteps of silence,
In buckets of gray water,
In piles of dirty rags.
White tile, black tile.
White tile, black tile.

ON THE SUBJECT OF DIRT

I am
the second cousin of dirt.
I step all over him.
He is a survivor—
playing the long game.
You are either part of him or
covered by him in the end.

He is unaware of his dry
sense of humor, or
how he makes us thirsty.
The world is his kingdom.
Mixed with the sky, he becomes dust.
With water, his name is Mud.

Dirt has a big heart.
You can see it when
the roses bloom,
the mountains form,
the stars fall.

SNAPSHOT STATUE

She stands in a forgotten corner,
Shy of visitors and silent.
She has been there so long,
Ferns grow around/between her feet.

She stares with sad, vacant eyes,
As time turns.
Her verdant corner,
From morning shadows to filtered afternoon.

Her polished terracotta skin,
Is taut over a stone-cold heart.
It beats in the rhythms of phantom rains.
She is only faithful to the water.

The vase in her hands,
Becomes heavy.
With the music she empties,
Into pools of private quiet.

Birds will swear they see her move.
Only the moon will love her smile.
Only the wind will kiss her lips.
She will never see her reflection.

DRUMS

I feel the steady drumming—inside my head.
The march begins—marchers long dead.
Their faces melt into haze and smoke
Like lost causes and forlorn hopes.
They float like hot ashes
       on evening's breeze,
Becoming ranks and files
flowing like rivers—rivers
       Flooded by mistakes made
Glorious with blood, bravery, and bones.
Bones that lay bleaching,
on the beaches,
in the bunkers,
at the bottom of the seas.
Against the cadence of precipitation,
       That lingers like anticipation,
The markers stand and wait.
       In lines, in rows, in silence—
Their white crosses flying tiny flags—
     Guardians of dreamless sleep.
I taste their footsteps
    on my tongue.
I smell their death
       like freshly cut grass.
I touch their screams:
As I walk between
the rows.
The rows that go on and on,

Like an ocean without a shore;
I can't even see
the horizon anymore.

Do you hear them?
The drums, their message,
The steady pulse.
It's the echo of heartbeats
Marching in cadence. Marching.

CIVIL WAR DIARY

July 17, 1863
My dearest,

I hope this letter makes it to you. Ezra and I are the only two who can write.

So we've been busy ever since we heard that we'll be in a big battle tomorrow. We're going
To capture this place called Fort Wagner.
It's been hot as hell since our ship arrived here, and
These wool uniforms don't help. Tomorrow, it won't matter.
I can't tell anybody—but I'm scared.
Being a sergeant, I can't show them how scared I am; but on the inside, I'm afraid. I try to keep thinkin' bout after
This is over, and we'll be free.
Free to love you, to hold you in my arms, to be together.
If I don't make it, make the boys
Learn how to read, so they can see these words and know that my last thoughts are of you and them. I expect no mercy tomorrow and will give none. May God forgive me.

July 19, 1863

It's the day after the battle, and my only thoughts are of you. I am lucky to be writing this letter. Before the battle, everyone was scared—not just me. They had a priest bless us in some foreign language, then the colonel of our regiment addressed us, telling everyone how he was sure we would do our duty, behave bravely—like men—and make Massachusetts proud. I wasn't so sure.

The bombardment only lasted five minutes, and we were sent in. The Rebs were waiting—untouched. Their first volley killed almost the whole front line. Ezra saw John the color guard slump to his knees and grabbed the flag by reflex.
I'll have to write a letter to his family in Boston next. We tried three times before the attack was canceled. If we were white soldiers, we would only have tried once.

The only way I can forget what I saw today is to think of your face smiling at me, the smell of your skin, the taste of your lips, and the sound of your laughter. I'm okay, I can sleep now. I *be comin' home,*

Comin' home. Hallelujah! I be comin' home.

Love,

D-DAY

I would wake
Within your arms
Watching you
Through half-closed eyelids.

But—I am here
Waiting for the jolt
As the ramp of my landing craft
Drops.
And I forget the dream.
Sounds: like a thousand tiny hammers
Echo off the steel
Becoming scarlet spots on human beings.
I escape over the side, into the surf.
The water's so cold
And I cannot hide.
My packs pull me under
Until I touch the sandy bottom.
And I am running—I don't know where.
Falling, crawling like a sea tortoise, trying to spawn
Trying to take one more deep breath
Trying to survive. Trying to find cover.

It will be like this:
I will arrive in your dream
Dressed in uniform.
We will sit in your garden
Telling stories, laughing, drinking tea.

I will reach for a pen
To write you a love note.
It will slip from my hand
Clatter to the stone pavers.
You will wake
Startled by the postman
Or Western Union
knocking on your door.

TIN SOLDIER TO THE PORCELAIN DOLL

Cool China / blue eyes hiding porcelain heart—
So beautiful and broken.
Do you see me standing at attention?
My eyes are on yours—not on the lethal
Bands of rubber that knock us down
Scatter us like chaff.
We surge ahead—irresistibly forward—
As if moved by invisible hands.

There are only a few of us left now
Protecting your perfection.
We gather together, awaiting
Your signal for our final charge.
If only you would nod your head
Or blink—so I would know you see me.

It is too late now.
I cannot see you—only the sky.
I do not feel the pain of my wounds
Only the emptiness of my desire.
It burns—yet I am so cold.
Is this what it's like
To have a porcelain heart?

TIN SOLDIER TO PORCELAIN DOLL— PART TWO

Hey, Baby! Where'd you get those big blue eyes?
Don't pretend you can't see me—
We're right next to each other.
That's right. I'm the one with the
Sharp red uniform and the bearskin cap.

I know some people would say I'm a little stiff.
Discipline and a wooden backbone make me this way.
If you want a contortionist, you can always go.
With G. I. Joe—if you've got an extra closet for
His accessories.

Some people would say I'm quiet
But I don't get paid to talk.
I stand guard against all the nuts in the world.
As for the matter of size—I am only three inches tall
But I have a bayonet
Which is more than Ken can claim.

Great, I see how it is—
Lay down and close your eyes
While I stand here at attention holding my gun.
Fine—be that way!
When you cry *mama*,
Don't expect me to change you.

BUTTERFLY BOY

"Once they took my picture," he says.
Coat opens at the bottom
Where the button
Was missing, like inside on his shirt
Or where his pants were pinned to size.
Those were the good days.
One war was over before another began.
Ice cream was a nickel, milk came in bottles.
And everyone liked "Ike."
He was eighteen, the summer
Vietnam got hot.
He exchanged his coat for camo green fatigues
A jungle full of hate and
Nightmares that only disappear
At the bottom of a bottle, the end of a needle.
The winter he returned
He found Jesus—or maybe
It was the other way around.
He learned to sing a gospel he couldn't read
Because it was warm inside.
In the spring, he rode the rails.
Working when he could, leaving when he would.
He rode buses, backseat blues, the same old news.
He came to the city, conquered a corner
Where he could sit and spit.
Everybody calls him "Butter"
As he glides down the street.
Smiling to angels of the fleet.

He flies in his own skies
Leaves us behind
As he sees the world
Through butterfly eyes.
"Once they took my picture," he says.

BATTLE OF THE
LONG GRASSES

We gather by the long grasses,
to feed our ponies and speak of peace.
We are so many in that place—
they come with so few.
They follow the river to find us.
The same way, a year ago,
they followed the river Washita to the
slaughtering of innocent women and children—
this they call victory.

We watch as they approach
blue uniforms, yellow-stripped legs.
We never intend to fight them.
There is no honor in unfair numbers.
We only ride out to slap them with our hands
count coup, send them away.
As we approach, they begin to shoot their horses.
They cannot be human—we need no mercy.
When the demon with the long golden hair falls—
It is face-first.
Each warrior, in turn, rides over the body.

It is quiet now, and we have moved on—
Only the long grasses and
the sound of the river remain.
This will be the story we tell.

White men will tell other tales.
Call us "savages,"
make treaties they will not keep
steal what they cannot own
Burn the rest.
We will only remember how blue the sky was
how the wind made the long grass dance.

KAMIKAZE INTENTIONS

My beloved,
Today, I will fly!
I will touch glory with my hand.
I will taste honor like honey.
Today I will fly and never land.

Listen closely,
and you will hear
The temple gong
sing my service
To the emperor.
Inhale, breathe deeply,
smell the incense burning
as I become the smoke.

Today,
I will let the sun,
the wind,
and the water,
Have all of me.
But my heart
belongs to you.

FEAR

It's not fear I feel,
more like fascination
freezing my attention
on the "just before"
of the banana peel.

It's not the sky I fear,
but my desire to fly,
while lacking wings or
my Icarus tendencies
as I begin to try.

It's not sleep I fear,
but nightmares that walk
leaving giant footprints
across the sky,
stranding me in the dark.

It's not the dark I fear,
keeping my eyes open wide
as imagination's dreams
dance to dirges in between,
and reality waits
on the other side.

It's not death I fear,
but the silence,
like thunder recalling

of when it was lightning,
now to be only
soft, gentle rain,
falling, falling down,
falling.

GIANTS

Some would say, "These hills and lakes were formed by glaciers."
Poor dead scientific minds—for I know different.

To the far right, the first rise is the head,
The next smaller humps are shield and body,
And the last two are the legs of the giants who fell here.

Their tribe, first old, their fight long forgotten,
Their purpose unknown, their pride erased.
They rest as they fell.

A small man marvels at their slumber,
Their snoring woods, laughing water,
Rolling nights, into eternal dreams,
One…second…at a time.
An arrogant man builds castles on their foreheads,
To get a better view.
A wealthy man takes the title of the land.
The man in love sees them not,
Because his eyes are on the stars, too small and far to hold.
A humble man listens, gently tapping his foot,
Wishing he could understand,
What's to gain in Afghanistan?

Somewhere, decisions are made,
By those that represent.
Another thirty thousand at the call of President.

Yet they can promise what they cannot keep,
A world of peace where children sleep.

So say a prayer, quiet waters,
For all our sons and all our daughters.
Let them know they're not alone,
Keep them safe and bring them home.

Don't get me wrong—but even giants cry.
Their tears, our lakes,
Their dreams, our sky,
Their courage, our song.

THE RALLY

One hundred thousand people
Came to hear him speak.
Flags were hung
Perfectly parallel to the pillars
That supported the podium
Where he would stand.
Torches were lit, and
When he appeared,
One hundred thousand voices
Cheered him as one.
He stood and stared at the crowd
Without saying a word
And stood there, and stood there—
For fifteen minutes.
At last, the crowd became quiet.
Then, and only then, did he begin to speak.
Softly at first, like a lover whispering
Of his passion for the country.

He spoke to the poor and promised them jobs.
He spoke to the middle class and promised them wealth.
He spoke to the wealthy and promised them power.
He spoke to the military and promised them guns.
He promised, "He alone" could make
The country, "Great again"—
And one hundred thousand voices cheered
As one hundred thousand right arms shot into the air.
What they didn't hear

Was the sound of breaking glass.
They didn't hear the sound of the hissing gas.
They didn't hear the screams of the burning books.
They didn't hear the children's frightened looks.
They just weren't listening.
Are we?

MIRROR

Stand in front of a mirror,
Lock eyes with your reflection.
Now, slowly, raise your right arm,
Straight out from your body,
Palm down, higher now,
Exhale as you salute,
Until your lungs are empty.
Now, hold that pose.
Do you feel the burning begin?
Deep inside, the lack of oxygen and buildup of CO_2,
Start to become toxic.
That's called the George Floyd feeling.
You want to breathe, but you're not allowed.

You'll start to notice pain in your shoulder,
The same, dull pain,
Felt by Rayshard Brooks,
When the first bullet impacted him
As he was running away.
He never felt the second one, only a feeling of relief,
As his soul left Atlanta.

It's only been a minute now, but
That's all it takes, one breath.
In less than one minute,
Breonna Taylor was hit by gunfire
Eight times—
In a case of mistaken identity.

Like so many that she treated,
Cared for, prayed for, cried for,
She passed—
Before the ambulance arrived.

Now you're feeling a little sick,
Like you might pass out and,
You hurt like things
Will never be better.
Yet, you're an American, and
You can't lower your salute,
Can't breathe—
What would people think?
Like the people who whine,
About the inconvenience of masks,
Never remembering a thousand people a day,
Who will never take another breath.

I want to put my arm down now,
Because I'm tired of all the excuses,
All the mistakes, all the lies.
But I'm afraid that if I do,
People might forget.
Forget about the ideals
That makes our nation great.
It's not about one person,
One party, one leader,
One color, one religion,
One god, or one way.
The greatness of our country
Is found in many different paths.
Many noble purposes, many precious freedoms,
Many precious lives.
Together, we are like facets of a diamond,
Each one a reflection of some shining hope within—
Some greater ideal.

Individually, we are shards of a broken mirror.
Each one, only a fragment of the complete picture,
Each one, jagged, sharp, and dangerous.

FROM THE CAPITOL BUILDING

I was born in a time of "No taxation without representation."
I stand for freedom, equality, justice for all.
I shelter the ideals of democracy.
I listen to debates of elected aristocracy.
I feel the heavy footsteps of liberty in infancy.

I was barely fourteen years old when the redcoats came,
Raping, pillaging, burning me—
Leaving me for dead.
Surviving, I vowed
That I would never let "that" happen again.
I became stronger,
Living through one war after another
Until I forgot all my fear, forgot all my pain,
Forgot all the darkness behind my closed doors.
I became a beacon of freedom.
What I didn't expect was the attack from within.
Where are my guards? My leaders?
Who will protect me?

They try to blind me now—one broken window at a time.
They hurt me, slamming and smashing my doors.
It's not my fault the doors were locked.
What was that—a gunshot?
They claim they love our country
While flying the flag of rebellion through my halls,

Attacking that which cannot defend itself.
Oh, Father Abraham, what have I done?
I'm so, so sorry.
Forgive me.
I only tried to be
what they wanted.

WORDS

I have heard:
"There is nothing to fear, but fear itself."
"To ask not; what your country will do for you,"
"It is America's destiny to put a man on the moon,"
"The president's been shot!"
I have heard dreams from a mountain,
With summits called liberty and equality.
I have heard: footsteps of first responders,
Rushing into crumbling towers
To rescue strangers
While others run away.
I have heard:
The cries of children/separated
who don't know why,
Mom and Dad are gone,
Or if they're coming back.

I have heard: "I am not a crook,"
And "I have sinned,"
While the truth runs by—
Very naked and very shy.
I have heard hostages,
And their captors, both prisoners of power,
Pawns in an unwanted war of the hour.

I hear silence in the halls of justice.
She listens to echoes of truth—
Bouncing blindly back and forth—

Like some lost soul,
Whispering its existence empty,
Shouting its frustration,
Wailing its lamentations
For this nation, this great nation,
This nation, indivisible.
Its tears form muddy footprints
On the black-and-white marble tile floor.

COWS VIEW ON POLITICS

They don't care—they don't vote, but
If they could vote, it would be like this:
There would be two bulls.

One bull would say the grass is greener in his pasture.
The other bull would say his grass is longer.
One bull will say that all cows are created equal.
And all should eat well.
The other bull will say: If the Bull is well-fed,
Then all the cows will be happy.
One bull would take down all the fences
And make the whole world his pasture.
The other bull wants his fences electrified,
And his horns sharpened to protect what's his.

Both bulls will agree to disagree—until the farm shuts down—
Because the farmer can't budget all the bull.
Finally, after much foot-stomping and galloping
Back and forth across the pasture—all at the farmer's expense—
The bulls will have their way with the cows and
The cows will vote—or they would if they could hold the markers.
The next morning: the farmer will still have cold hands.
The bulls will have their own pasture with free health care
And a nontaxable retirement account, again, all paid for by the farmer
And the cows?
They will be left with the BS and the same old grass as yesterday.

TOGETHER

Together,
we watch
         as clouds
         gather
tornadoes of
         dust in the distance.
     We lose
         our way in the woods,
play games until
         the sun goes down.
We share first cigarettes,
     split bottles of cheap wine,
pass joints while laughing,
     lying on our backs in the grass.
We talk to the stars—
     about the futures they will have:
Listen—as heartbeats measure
         the present becoming past.
We pile spring on summer,
         on autumn,
         on winter,
barely noticing the extra weight,
     or how the days become shorter—
like the steps
and breaths we take.
Together.

SIGNS

We are signers—forming words with our fingers.
We are signers—touching lips with our hands
To say thank you for the small change
You kept in your pocket.
Touching lips to say, "Goodnight," "Goodbye,"
"Hello," or "Stay with me."
Touching lips to silence the anticipation
Of the next quiet moment
That has already passed to the next.
Like songs from our souls,
We remember the melody, but not the words,
We remember the beat, but not the meaning.
Players in the park
Chase the orange-colored ball,
Above
Rusty rims dressed in chains,
Attached to a painted white backboard mistress.
She rattles like a tin can behind the "Just Married" sign,
As prayers get answers by sweat and slam,
Or cut and jam.
"No look" or "No game" until
The city turns off the lights—
Leaving the blind man on the bench
Listening:
To the echoes of sneakers on asphalt,
The fading wail
Of another ambulance,
The chorus of

Police sirens
Singing in off; beat
Harmony,
The tolling of the
Church bell signaling
Another day.
A trembling hand
Makes the sign of the cross.
How dark is it—outside?

SHADOWS

My pen
is a shadow
falling on words.
Dripping
ink-stained branch—
it touches memories
like fingers
flipping pages
of a favorite book.

It knows so little of what it writes
exhausting its life
in handwritten sacrifice
until silent and dry
as a hollow husk.
It is forgotten.

In some dark corner
of some old desk
she sleeps and dreams
of our first touch
waiting for her second chance
to tell the stories
to do the dance.

THE RED DOOR

When I came to the theater,
I was very young.
They brought me to the largest dressing room
and hung a star on me.
They said it was because I was good
at keeping secrets in
and out.
Secrets like the bottle in the bottom drawer
or the pills in the silver boxes in front of the mirror, and
oh, I would never tell about the odor
of burning rope and incense
or how the director used me
as his vertical casting couch.
I was the door to success.

Maybe it was because I knew too much,
or maybe it was the splinters I left behind.
But now I'm at the backstage alley door.
Painted red and poster,
I announce last month's performance
to the homeless and the addicts in need
of shadow or shelter from the city,
to light a cigarette / catch their breath.
I've gotten used to the smell,
but I sure miss my star.

WALKERS

They move,
heads down,
singing to the light boxes
in their hands.
They have almost the identical gait
as a conspiracy of ravens.
They use to look up—
Singing the goodness of the day, the sky,
to each other.
Now, they are obsessed with
the moving pictures in their paws.
They don't even notice the pigeons
Begging on the roadside.
Sometimes, the boxes sing back,
but the walkers don't always like the song.
I have seen many a light box trying desperately
to learn to fly—
only to fail, fall, become silent.

There was a time
when the walkers lived in trees,
with/like us—safe from the predators below.
Gradually, they climbed down,
traveled
farther and farther from the safety of the forest.
When they returned,
we watched in horror
as they sacrificed the trees to fire,

warming their featherless bodies.

We watch as they kill one another.
Not for food,
but because one was a different color,
or one sings a different song,
or because one
worships God in his own way.
Claiming life is precious, and God is good,
they kill to prove they are right and to prove that
God loves us all equally.

They claim civilization like a birthright, ignoring
the suffering that surrounds them.
Still, they walk on.
Only the old remember the songs
they learned from us so long ago.
Perhaps, they will sing for forgiveness
to the forests they destroy.
Perhaps, we will add our tears to the rain.
Perhaps, when the sun shines,
the desert will drink our pain.

PEEKING

The dead are peeking.
Perhaps it's the boom of the cannon
or the *pop, pop* of musket fire
that disturbs their sleep.
Or perhaps, it's the desire
to see the outcome of the battles
they fight and refight,
seeking to understand the outcome—
That is always the same—
Or to tally the numbers
the way the living keep score,
or to estimate the time that has passed
that they no longer have to spend,
so the ground may surrender their souls,
so they may be reborn—
oblivious of past and future.

The dead are peeking.
To check on us—the—
To make sure we don't forget them.
To make sure we don't forget what it was all about.
Don't forget—the promises, the treaties,
the old ways, the tears, the cost.

The dead are peeking,
Looking for signs that it's okay to join the living once again.
It's okay to share, to laugh, to love, to feel—
That they are needed once again,

That it's time to shake off the dirt,
Stand up and be counted,
That it's time to pose for the pictures,
That it's time to smell the wood fires,
Talk about what they've learned.

The dead are peeking.
Do you see them?

OCEAN'S MIST

The ocean's mist
Drifts ashore
Like sailors, seaweed,
And tides.
The air is filled with the smell,
Like a stranger
In a small town.
Gull choirs
Shriek their hallelujahs
In dissonant chords.
As church bells
Toll the hour.
Early risers look
For a sunrise disguised
In a mask of fog.
Fishermen begin the day
In hip boots and nets.
Always eager with anticipation,
While dogs bark
The daily news,
Children begin their play
Screaming their existence
Into reality.
Old men watch and listen
From comfortable chairs,
Tell stories of their youth,
Drink to forget their age,
Burn off the fog.

HOW DO WE KNOW?

How do we know the truth,
When the obvious is obscured,
The absolute is relative and
No one really knows what's going on?
When what is said yesterday is tomorrow's lie,
When innocent people have to die
To make us wonder how,
To make us wonder why.
Like when did trust
Becomes a bank account,
Or honesty a sign of weakness?
Or empathy for
Your fellow man
Become a sign of meekness?

We stand at crossroads
Where words and actions
Meet ideas and ideals.
Down one road is destruction,
Degradation, and the death of a dream.
The other road is uphill,
With many obstacles, yet unseen.
Together, we can share compassion.
Together, we can overcome oppression.
Together, we can change obstacles into triumph.
Together, we can do anything.

UNSINKABLE

When they found her—
     Bow buried,
     Sixty-five feet deep,
Into the North Atlantic floor.
     She had a mile-long trail of debris,
          Like the tail of a comet.
Through a sky made of water,
     Two miles down.

Her nine decks collapsed.
Her grand staircase leading to,
          Nowhere.
And everywhere,
     Pairs of empty shoes,
Silent monuments,
     to those with no lifeboats.

Now like a thousand *Titanics*,
     Ramming icebergs of reality,
Oil gushes from a well of unprepared,
     Fifty thousand barrels a day,
Like no one even cared.

We are:
     Millions of pairs of empty shoes,
     Staring at a blackened shoreline.
We are:
     An endless staircase looking for an exit.

We are:
    Sinking and cannot swim.
We have no lifeboats.
We have no lifeboats.
We have no lifeboats.

THE ASTRONAUT'S REPLY

(UPON DISCOVERING, A TRIP TO THE STARS WOULD
INCLUDE ONE THOUSAND DAYS OF SUSPENDED ANIMATION.)

How could I dream
      For a thousand days—
  Without you.
When just one second is eternity lost.
My mind knows no such measures.
As demanded by the heart,
It reinvents space
      Divided by time/light,
      Tries to invert proportions
In a flux of quantum theory,
    Grabbing at ideas while
        Feeling rejected by the stars—
        Only to Icarus fall
        Short of all.

        All this is,
        It's all that matters;
        Yet,
        The present is
        Still flattering truth
    With promises of future fame.
    The past stands,
In the corner,
      Quietly unobserved,
  Like Alice in Wonderland,

Looking glass in one hand,
Hookah in the other,
Her tears watering flowers on the wall.
So tell me, please,
How could I sleep through all of this,
Let alone dream?

BENCH BY THE LAKE

Old man and wife
Experiment with retirement.
He smokes his discomfort
With her conversation.

She never tires of listening to his
Grunting nonreplies.
It's motivation
To walk a little more
With this stranger.

His labor made a home,
Vacations, meals, cars, plans.
His snoring kept her awake at night.
Sitting next to her
On the bench by the lake,
He holds her hands,
Always cold in October,
Waiting for winter.

He smiles—
A smile lost in the glare
Reflecting off the water.
He lights another cigarette.
Painfully rising/offering his arm/
Walking some more—
Because she likes that.

ABOUT THE AUTHOR

Born in Concord, New Hampshire, and raised in Caribou, Maine, Stephen Redic is a true New England product. An avid sports fan, historian, musician, and writer, Stephen maintains an active lifestyle. Describing himself as "the luckiest guy who never won the lottery," fortune has smiled on Stephen with everything from meeting every President since Eisenhower, to beating cancer twice, to being a great-grandfather—six times! All these blessings combined with the good fortune of being adopted by two loving parents, who did everything possible to provide a good life, and then being reunited—at the age of forty-five—with his birth family give Stephen a wealth of experience to draw on. Living in Candia, New Hampshire, Stephen is surrounded by nature and friends.